SO, YOU HAVE A BAND

SO, YOU HAVE A BAND

An insider's guide to developing, growing, and presenting your band as serious business

TIM WENGER

Inkwell Media Services
Lakewood, CO

CONTENTS

1.

SO, YOU HAVE A BAND?

Introduction

You have a band. The time spent on practicing, the money spent on gear, and the parents/roommates/significant others annoyed during the learning process are all about to be worth it. You met some people, or came together with a group of friends, and formed a group. Are you going to be the next big thing? Probably not. Save yourself the massive disappointment and let go right now of the delusion of grandeur that all new bands have. This is the digital age, the time when every musician has an album and bands with minimal talent are headlining theaters solely because they are masters of marketing and have a lot of friends.

The greatest challenge about being in a band is that while it's easy to be *in* one, it's hard to *do well* in one. It's a path where the journey is the destination. What happens along the way, and how your group reacts to it, will determine how long you survive and ultimately how successful you are. There is going to be conflict between friends. There is going to be resentment. There is going to be no money. Are you down?

But in no way does that mean that it isn't possible to 'live the dream' a little bit, even if it only lasts for a few years. Being successful as a musician does not mean you have to become a millionaire because of it. In fact, as you start playing gigs and becoming part of a local music scene, your definition of 'making it' as a band might change completely. No matter what your goals and ambitions are as a musician, you have to start at the beginning — be willing to put yourself out there. If you want people to take you seriously (and I'm guessing that you do, since you're taking the time to read this), presenting your band, act, or group as professionally as possible is key. You want people to think you have it together right? It actually isn't that hard to do, it just takes time and effort.

I've worked for four years as the Managing Editor of a monthly music industry print magazine, as a talent buyer at a 500-cap club in Denver, and toured the western United States as the guitarist in a ska-punk band a fair amount over the past decade. I am going to get straight to the point in this book. My goal is for you, the reader, to have an overwhelming amount of actionable advice that can be discussed with your group and worked on. I lived everything I talk about in these pages and I'll be the first to admit I made mistakes along the way. Hopefully, my advice will help your group avoid those same missteps.

Over the years my perspective on what it means to be a successful musician changed a lot. I used to think that I was destined to be a rocker, to tour full time and never have to work a day job again. While this proved false, it certainly didn't mean that I failed in my quest. Through playing music, I have had the opportunity to go on multiple out-of-state tours, played shows opening for many of the bands I grew up listening to, and made some of the best friends I will ever have.

To be honest, it didn't happen at all like I thought it would. When I started playing in bands, social media was just becoming a thing. No one yet knew the huge impact platforms like Myspace, Facebook, and SonicBids would have on the way independent bands conduct business. The idea of building a profile or having an electronic press kit was a relatively new concept and registering as an S-Corp with a business checking account was completely foreign to all four of us. The important thing to remember when doing ANYTHING that is putting you or your music out there is to consider what the person viewing you is going to think.

In this book, I will break down the steps to achieving growth for your group by going over necessary actions that are often overlooked by newer local-level bands. The type of stuff that might not seem important right off the bat but makes all the difference in how serious you appear to those looking at you. Having your act together how willing people are to work with you, from promoters and talent buyers to the media.

Here in Chapter 1, we'll cover the first back-of-house steps your band should take after forming, before concentrating on front-of-house steps. We're not going to talk about writing songs or figuring out how many people should be in the band. We're not going to talk about buying gear. Figure that stuff out with your crew. Once the dust has settled and you have a few months of band practice under your belt, you'll start thinking beyond the basement. This is the kick off point.

Note: *I am going to talk over and over again about the concept of 'professionalism.' I don't want anyone to get the wrong idea and think that I am implying that you can't have any fun and that everything you do should be business-centric. Playing music is supposed to be fun, and playing shows is supposed to be even more fun. They are if you do them the right way. When talking about professionalism, I am talking about having your ducks in a row in two equally important but very different way: back-of-house and front-of-house.*

Back-of-house

The best advice I can give is to make sure everyone is on the same page as far as what the band is doing and what it wants to do. This is a huge reason why weekly meetings are amazing. Everyone can get on point, and hold each other accountable for being professional and not sloppy, on time and not late, on point and not drunk, and make sure everyone is doing their part. This will help you avoid unnecessary drama and keep the good times going.

Band member responsibilities and band agreements

Bands are like a family. This is both a good and bad thing — just like any family, everyone wants to feel important and included in the decision-making. In most band situations people will get upset, jealous, and hold grudges if one person is calling all the shots and the other members have no say. If you are starting a band yourself and are hiring musicians to play your songs, you can hold those rights. But if everyone is contributing to the songwriting, arranging their schedule to accommodate practices and gigs, and helping out with any financial costs, they each deserve an equal say.

It is important to hold regular band meetings to ensure everyone is on the same page. This can easily be done either before or after practice, with an agenda to cover any pending gigs, upcoming schedule issues, or any other questions that arise. So many bands break up because they fail to communicate well. Expect that everyone won't always agree on everything. You may want to set a 'democracy' rule in your band where everyone gets a vote and in the event of a tie, a discussion ensues or an outside party is consulted. This can be used for decisions regarding songwriting, whether or not to take a gig, or just about anything else that arises.

As you reach a point where you are recording music and selling it, buying merchandise to sell at gigs, and making even a small amount of income from your shows, it is a good idea to have everyone sign a formal Band Agreement. (View a sample band member agreement in the Appendix of this book.)

That way it is on paper how funds will be distributed and who owns the band. Make sure you have a contingency in place in case a member leaves the group and someone else is brought in. The agreement should also cover what each band member's role is within the group, other than playing his or her instrument. Here are some common roles that you will need to fill:

- **Booking/contact person:** When dealing with venues, media, and anyone else, it is best to have a point person in the group to serve as the main contact. This will help establish consistency and it is important that the people and places you work with know who to call for bookings, media inquiries, etc.
- **Design/social media person:** Is the drummer a whiz at Photoshop, or does he have thousands of social media followers? This person should be in charge of managing the band's social media accounts and web presence, as well as designing a logo, show posters, merch, etc.
- **Transporting gear/driver:** When you first start, you likely won't have a van or any specified band vehicle. Hopefully, one or more of the group has an SUV or a car with a large trunk. If not, get this situation dialed in before you start booking gigs. If you are not going to split the driving equally, one member's role can be as the main driver. It is good to have someone pegged as the late night driver for after gigs, or long drives between towns if you get to the point of touring.
- **Manager/clutch decision maker:** Often this person will be the contact person as well, but a quick note on

this: typically, having a mom or dad be the manager is not a good idea. Having a 'mom-ager' or 'dad-ager' is a great way to get laughed at by venues. For local bands, having a 'manager' other than an active band member is usually a bad idea because often that person has no idea what they are doing and is completely unnecessary. If you aren't making money as a band and the members aren't too busy focusing on playing music full-time, you don't need a manager.

- Speaking from the talent buyer's perspective, it is really annoying when a local group wants me to deal with their 'manager' when all I want to do is book them for an upcoming local gig. I know the band is a local group and not traversing the country for a living. Ego gets you nowhere in the music business, so never act like you are too big of a deal or too busy to have a conversation with someone. Typically, this just slows down the process and makes venues less likely to call you back because they don't want to be given the runaround. Having a 'manager' does not in any way make your band look better. The best local bands are the ones that can handle themselves and be professional, not pass the work on to someone else.

Do you have a name?

This seems so simple. The name should just come to you, right? After jamming for a few weeks *something* has got to pop into your heads. That perfect few words that sums up who you are. The key here is FEW WORDS. As little as one word can do the trick. You want it to be memorable but also not annoying to anyone who will be writing it down or typing it up on a show poster. Believe it or not, there are bands who gig at the venue I work at with ten letter names. Very unique, but extremely hard to list on our website, fit onto a ticket, or recite to someone over the phone when they call and ask who is playing tonight. I wouldn't be surprised to learn that the band members themselves get tired of repeating and explaining such a long name. You will be doing everyone including yourselves a favor by having a relatively simple band name. It may not easily come to you, but often just coming up with something intended to be temporary will do the trick. My bandmates and I certainly never intended for Oatie Paste to be our long time name. At first, it was just something we told friends that we'd use until we thought of something better, but once we got out onto the show circuit and got some stickers printed out it was too late to change it. Nine years later and I am convinced it has a nice ring to it (and what better way to describe to your girlfriend over the phone what oatmeal should look like when finished? True story).

Making the band a business

Once everyone has their back-of-house roles figured out, consider forming an LLC or for-profit corporation. These days, the process of becoming a business is relatively painless. In most states, it can be done online by filling out a form with the Secretary of State. Each state has their fee and requirements. In Colorado, for instance, there is a $50 fee to register a business. Figure out whether an LLC or for-profit Corporation is the best route for you. If you choose the corporation route, filing as an S-Corp is the standard route. Here is a basic breakdown of the similarities and differences between both entities.

Similarities

They both offer limited liability protection. This means that the individuals who own the company cannot be personally held responsible for debts or liabilities. So, if you take out a loan to buy a tour van and for whatever reason, your company defaulted on that loan, it would not affect your personal credit. This does not mean it's a free-for-all, though; if you screw someone over and owe them money or services, they can still take legal action against the company and put you in front of a judge. If the company owes money, it is always best to pay that money back.

Same goes for what your band (company) agrees to do; If you sign a contract with a venue or promoter for a certain service, say a 90-minute set with a 15-minute set break, you'll want to honor that. While you likely won't be sued if you only play for 82 minutes, word of mouth travels fast in this industry.

Both LLCs and S-Corps have what is called Pass-Through Taxation. This means that business profit or loss is passed through to the individual owner's tax returns. S-Corps always file a business tax return, while LLCs only file a business tax return if the company has more than one owner (if you are a band, you'll need to file a business tax return.)

Differences

For musicians, a notable difference between the two lies in the transferability of ownership. Corporations have stock (In the case of a band, you will generally create one share for each member and perhaps the manager, if you have one. This gives each person equal voting rights.) and this stock is freely transferable. This means that in the instance of a member leaving and being replaced by someone else, the share of the company can easily be transferred to the new person if that is the route you decide to take. With LLCs, membership interest (a share of ownership of the company) is generally not freely transferable. All voters must be in approval before making a change. In many circumstances, this won't matter much, but if your band has to kick out a member who does not want to go, this may cause a problem.

Avoiding future problems

I watched a band I know quite well go through a situation where a member of the LLC left the group and was replaced. After he left, the band had an opportunity to give rights of one of their previously recorded songs, on which the former member played guitar, to a company that wanted to use it in a television commercial. The former member was against this and because he legally had a say in what happened to the song, they were not able to have their song used in the commercial. This despite the fact that the former member would have received his share of royalty payments from the use of the song.

Issues like this are all too common in bands. Even those

who start out as best friends are likely to endure some type of hardship or disagreement about proceedings of the group. The most important thing to keep in mind when forming your business is what will happen if a member leaves. This should be discussed before any papers are signed. Ideally, all members will agree to give up their voting right if they leave the band, while still maintaining the right to any royalty payments due to them for their services while in the band. This is a pretty easy thing to work out if everyone agrees to it early on, and drawing up a document outlining the plans for such an instance is highly recommended. I'm not a lawyer, so a quick chat with one or a quick google search of band documents can offer further advice here.

Choosing a bank

Once you are a registered business, you can open a bank account, apply for a loan, and enjoy any other benefits. In the instance that the venue would like to pay you by check, it can be made out to the business and deposited or cashed at the bank no problem.

- When choosing a bank, my personal advice is to select a small bank you can develop a relationship with. Look for one with a strong business banking program — a quick search online should provide some good leads in your area. While Wells Fargo has thousands of convenient ATM locations all over the country, they could give a shit about you and your business. The same goes for other mega-banks.
- Getting to know the personal banker you open your

account with is crucial not only on the surface but for things like getting a loan or having overdraft fees reversed. Small banks need your business. It is easier to get that person on the line in an emergency and easier to get honest feedback about which way you should go when making financial decisions. In Colorado, I use Vectra Bank. They approved us for a $5000 loan to buy a van after a larger bank would not, and every time I go in they remember my name and ask how the band is doing. Little things like that are nice.

Front-of-house

Front-of-house means on social media, at shows, with your merch, anything that is seen by the general public. You want to create a 'brand' for your band. What style of music do you play? What comes to mind when you think about the most successful bands in that genre? Is it their dress style, the drug of choice of their fans, their music videos? All of these things are a result of the band's image. Popular bands represent something to their fans, inspiring a desire to be like them. This is true from the pretty image of pop stars like Justin Bieber down to the dirtiest, grittiest metal bands – fashion and style are huge in the music business.

- Do a photoshoot. If you aren't willing or can't pay for a professional photographer, use your network to find a friend or family member who is a decent shooter and set up a meeting to come up with a theme. Use these photos on social media, in your electronic press kit, and other situations when corresponding with professionals in the industry.

- What do you want people to think of when they see your band live or visit your website? Part of the fun of creating a band is that you get to decide how you want to present yourselves. No matter what you do, be sure to keep it consistent across the board.
- While you may not want to be identified with just one style of music, people need to be able to label you as something. Over and over, you will be asked what style of music you play and if you don't have a solid answer, what motivation will anyone have to want to check you out?
- As far as the live performance aspect goes, the audience wants to identify with you or relate to you somehow, and they expect that feeling to be the same at the next show and the one after that. It is important to keep your vibe the same at each show. When someone describes your group to another person there is something tangible to be said and understood. If the bass player does all of the talking between songs at one gig and the drummer does the talking at the next, people will get confused.
- If you incorporate humor into your set, do it at every show and deliver it in the same manner. Bands that joke around and have a good time on stage are much more enjoyable to watch than those who simply introduce the next song and dive right in.

It may seem like this is hard to do, but it just takes practice. I always recommend that bands play a couple of house parties or other low-key gigs before stepping onto a bigger stage at a venue, just to get their feet under them a bit. The first time you're playing in front of someone can be quite a nerve-wracking experience.

Party image

Being in a band is much more than just showing up, drinking beer, and playing shows. If someone has no interest in doing more than that, kick them out of the band immediately (or make them read this book – they'll either figure it out or realize they are wasting everyone's time). Many successful bands put up the image that they party all the time, that it's always so much fun and they have it all figured out. This is not the case. The constant images of bands partying on tour and some kind of leisurely life is a front designed to brand their image. Any band that can't be professional in public situations, and is always drunk and out of control, is never going to go anywhere and will not attract any fans.

If you are blacked out onstage, no one is going to like you. That scene already happened. Save the excessiveness for after you leave the venue. This is something that took me and my group quite a while to figure out. My most embarrassing moment as a musician came at our first CD release party in 2008. We headlined a local club where we regularly played and knew the staff, the owner, and most of the people in the crowd. Short story, we drank too much before taking the stage and while on-stage, and ended up getting cut off by the sound guy about 2/3 of the way through our set. I was extremely embarrassed to go back into that club the next time. Luckily, we maintained a strong relationship with the venue. We promoted the hell out of that show and the place was packed. Even though we underperformed on stage, the door and the bar did great sales for the night. We were asked back after promising never to black out again.

I learned a lot that night. I'll admit, these days I still enjoy raising a toast to the crowd. The only difference is that it isn't my 20th toast of the night. Running the business of a band is actually quite enjoyable when taken seriously and done correctly; there is so much pride that goes into building something yourself and putting it out there for other people to see and enjoy. For me, that has always been part of the thrill of being in a band. Taking a concept and making it a reality. That, in itself, is both professional and fun.

2.

HOW TO BOOK SHOWS AND PRESENT YOURSELF PROFESSIONALLY

You've got your group together, have some songs written and have worked out some kinks. The group has been playing the songs for a few months now and everyone feels comfortable, maybe even anxious for the next step of putting yourselves out there in front of an audience. But how do you make it happen? If you are just starting out in your town's scene, there is a good chance you don't know anyone at any of the local bars or venues. That's ok, getting yourself a gig (hopefully a slew of them!) is actually not very hard to do.

First, there are several things that are important to have in order. The road to rocking-out is just getting started! I know how exciting and nerve-wracking it is to prepare for the first actual gig. Your mom might be there! Your friends might be there! The last thing you want to do is embarrass yourself!

One thing I'll say that my band did a good job of is having our set well-rehearsed before we ever played our first show. We had the set list written out, and I wore my favorite shirt (It was a brown polo shirt. Looking back, pretty dorky. I'm pretty sure I looked like a golfer instead of a rocker, but oh well.) To make the experience more enjoyable for everyone, check the following things off the list before that big night happens.

Do you have your songs down?

- You want to impress people, right? You want them to tell you after the show that they enjoyed your music and are looking forward to next time. Playing gigs is incredibly fun and a good way to stroke the artistic ego. But not if the bass player is playing in the wrong key and the drummer keeps stopping in the middle of the song because he is playing the chorus instead of the verse.
- I know that everyone in the band is so excited to get onstage in front of a crowd, put your left foot up on the monitor like your favorite band does, listen to cheers and accept free beer when packing up. But if your band doesn't know your set like the back of your hand, then not only are there countless bands doing it better than you, there is also not much of a shot at you being asked

to open up for that touring act you sound like next time they come through town. Practice, practice, practice.

- Personally, I've always enjoyed band practice. Laughing and joking with the crew while hanging out in a basement playing music and drinking PBR after work is pretty damn fun.
- When you have it down and are ready to step out into the world, book your first show a couple months down the line. Play a couple house parties or barbecues first to get your feet wet. That way, you can work out any kinks and impress the bar staff at the local club right away.

Who is the point person in your band?

Like we discussed earlier, one person in the group should be responsible for reaching out to venues. Everyone can share their opinions, but talent buyers find it very annoying when multiple members of a group hit them up and ask the same questions. The rest of this chapter primarily deals with action items for the point person in the band.

Finding a venue

Now, let's find a good venue. Where do other local bands of similar style play in your town? Maybe there is an open mic or a certain night of the week that that venue tries out new acts? How should you contact them? Most venues have booking information on their website. Some will have a form right there online to fill out asking for links, a bio, and other info so that they can schedule your group appropriately. Others will just have an email or phone number listed. When reaching out to a venue, there are a few things to keep in mind:

Your draw

The number of people you can bring out to see you at a show is known as your band's draw. Typically, the bands playing the best nights and the best time slots are not only good bands, but they have a strong draw. The most important factor for any bar or club is whether or not your band can get people in the door to watch your show. No matter how good you are, if no one comes out to your show, you are not going to be re-booked very often (if at all).

Venues stay in business by selling beer, and they need people in the door to buy that beer. The more beer they sell during your set, the better show you are going to be offered next time around. Believe me, venue staff notice these things. Most clubs keep a database of what each band draws to each show, and they book their future shows based on these numbers.

Even if you are a young band and are playing an all ages club it is still important to work hard on getting people to your show. Each person in the group should be responsible for bringing at least five people to every show at first, and more as your band grows and plays out. This is why it is important not to book shows too close together– your friends, family, coworkers, fans, whatever, are not going to come watch you play every weekend. They will, though, be excited to come watch you play one well-promoted show every month or two, and if you are any good, they might even start bringing *their* friends!

Promotion

When talking with a talent buyer or promoter, always emphasize that you can bring people out to watch you and then actually do it. Some clubs ask in their booking form 'Why will people come watch you' or 'Why should we book you.' This is a perfect time to let the talent buyer know that you can bring people in to buy drinks. If cold calling or emailing, it is not inappropriate at all to disclose this information. There is no need to bullshit them and say you can bring 100 people out if you can't do it. If you can't bring anyone, don't book a show. Be honest, if you can bring twenty or thirty friends and coworkers, most clubs that deal with local music will be more than willing to work with you.

Note: *The myth of the 'built-in crowd' is exactly that – a myth. Do not approach shows thinking that bringing your crowd is not important, that the venue has people there already and it's just your job to get up and play your songs. If your group wants to become a classic rock cover band that plays four-hour sets at cougar bars, then perhaps the built-in crowd can become a reality for you. But if you are playing your own songs, trying to grow your own brand and progress as musicians, promotion is key.*

More info about dealing with talent buyers and promoters

A talent buyer is someone who books and organizes

concerts for a venue. The biggest thing to keep in mind when dealing with them is that this is likely either their full-time job or a part-time gig that they take very seriously. Even though your band is new and it may not be anything more than a hobby to you, to these guys and other people who work at a music venue, this is their job and they want to deal with people who take gigging seriously. Leave a good impression and they'll be calling *you* for shows instead of the other way around.

Do you have a stage plot?

A stage plot is a description of your band's set up for use by a sound engineer during your show. It contains information such as the number of people in the band and which instruments are located where on stage, how many inputs your group will need to be plugged into the sound board, and any funky things about your setup that they need to know about. A good way to impress a talent buyer is to send a stage plot over after you are confirmed for a show.

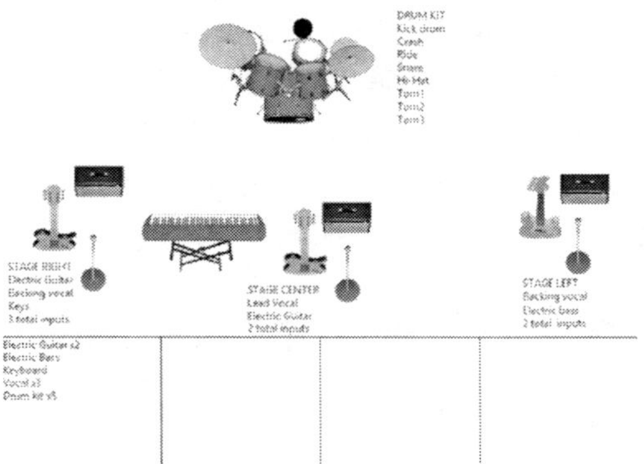

Sample Stage Plot

We're booked! Now what?

Congratulations! Playing gigs will likely be one of the most rewarding experiences you will ever have. Let's make sure you have all the information necessary to do it right.

What does the club expect of you as far as promotion? Will you need to design a show poster and send it to them or will they do that for you? Are there pre-sale tickets? (This is when the club prints your band a stack of tickets and gives them to you to sell before the show, you then return the cash and any unsold tickets when you arrive at the club. This is very typical for bigger clubs and shows with larger headliners. On many local nights, this may not be necessary).

Do you have all of the information about the night? Who else is playing? What time will you play? When is load in, is there a sound check or will you be line checking before your set? How will you be getting paid? Often, this information will be sent to you in what is called an 'Advance.' Typically sent via email within one month of the show, an Advance will lay out all specifics of the gig including who to contact with any further questions. Again, this may not always happen on local shows, so it doesn't hurt to ask for this information during the booking process.

Dealing with staff at the show

Typically, your point person will want to check in with the sound guy when you arrive at the venue. He will instruct you on when and where to load in.

What should I do if we have to cancel a gig?

The short answer: have a damn good reason, especially if it is day-of-show. Your band not being there will throw a loop in the production schedule and also means that there will be fewer people in attendance. Both of these are not good, but if handled professionally, you shouldn't ruin the relationship with the club. Let the talent buyer know as soon as possible. Don't bother making up an excuse. The venue has heard every reason imaginable for canceling a show, so save face and just be honest.

More info on gigging can be found in chapter 5, where we talk about which gigs to take, which ones to turn down, and how often to book.

3.

APPROACHING AND DEALING WITH BLOGS AND THE MEDIA

Hypothetical situation here. You are in a band with two other guys that were polar opposites. One guy takes the business of the band as seriously as any other aspect of his life. He works hard not only at practice but also behind the scenes. Inviting his friends and family to shows, assisting with online and street promotion, and wearing whatever hat is necessary to help the band out. The other guy writes great songs. Beyond that, he wants nothing to do with anything other than showing up and playing. He never promotes, only brings his girlfriend to the shows, and leaves immediately after we got offstage, leaving the drummer and myself to load the gear from the van back into our practice spot at the end of the night. Which person do you think is a more valuable band mate?

It always surprises me how many people don't realize the amount of effort it takes to make progress as a musician. As we discussed earlier, each member of the band should have a back-of-house role. It is up to the band members to hold each person accountable for the responsibilities. Think of your band as a sort of mastermind group, at each meeting or practice, each member should report on how things are going in their 'department.'

That way, everyone will have that extra bit of motivation because no one wants to be humiliated in front of the rest of the crew. Not having your homework done when the teacher calls on you never felt very good, right? Being that kid certainly isn't the cool thing to do when you and your friends are working together towards a common goal. Set manageable goals to accomplish before the next practice, whether that be to design a show poster, follow up on a gig lead, or brainstorm a list of promo ideas for the next show.

One of the tasks that should be assigned to a member of the group is approaching and dealing with the media. There are a million different blogs, magazines, and Facebook pages dedicated to independent music and here in this chapter, we will go over how to approach them professionally and how to handle interviews, how to put together an electronic press kit, and what to do once you have received media coverage.

Research the appropriate person to contact at the publication

- Music media can be a great help in promoting a big show, record release, or another milestone. The first thing you need to do is research the appropriate outlets to contact. Does your town have a weekly alternative newspaper with a music section? How about online blogs and digital magazines that cover music in your area or genre? A quick web search will turn up numerous outlets that may be relevant to you and are already reaching your potential fan base.
- If you or your group are doing something newsworthy like releasing new music, kicking off a tour or playing a big show, appropriate media outlets will want to know about it. It is their job to keep their readers informed of what is going on. Before reaching out to them, make sure you have these things in order:
- What's their email address? As a magazine editor, I personally despised getting cold phone calls from musicians or their management/PR teams. A well-timed email with a press release, hi-res photo, and any information explaining why the band/show/record is relevant to our publication's readership, on the other hand, is always welcomed and encouraged. When I did receive a cold call I would typically request the caller to put the info into an email and send it to me that way. If you cannot identify a specific person, find the submissions, news tips, or general contact email. Typically, a publication will have this stuff listed in a

'Contact' section or will have a specific link set up to submit news tips and press releases.

- To best get an editor's attention, having a strong headline is key! He or she does not want to read 'local band looking for coverage.' Make it catchy and exciting! Most important, spell everything correctly, use appropriate capitalization but avoid writing in all caps. Here is a sample headline and email body:

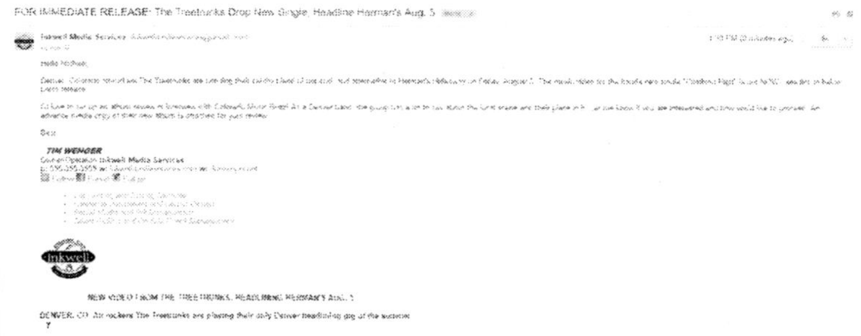

FOR IMMEDIATE RELEASE: The Treetrunks Drop New Single, Headline Herman's Aug. 5

TIM WENGER

View the full text of this email in the Appendix.

Draft a press release containing the following:

- In the email's subject line, write "FOR IMMEDIATE RELEASE:" before your headline. For example, a good subject line reads "FOR IMMEDIATE RELEASE: Durango Ska Band Oatie Paste to release new EP December 15." Include something that immediately identifies something relevant to that publication, such as a location, certain venue, genre, or whatever it is that the publication frequently writes about. Do some research and you will have a much higher chance of success if you have a basic understanding of what the publication is looking to cover.

- Intro paragraph with all relevant info on the newsworthy topic (an upcoming show, record release, whatever it is you are doing).
- 2nd and 3rd paragraph with background info on the project/show and all other relevant details pertaining to it (who else is playing, why you are so excited, why anyone should care).
- Boilerplate paragraph – your band's bio/history, a list of notable accomplishments.
- A high-res photo and links to all applicable social media and web pages.
- At the very bottom: For media inquiries, contact (member name) at (phone number) or (email).

View the text of this press release in the Appendix.

If the media outlet replies, they will likely either request more information or ask for an interview. If they do not respond, it typically means they did not feel the information you submitted them was of use to their audience. Do not take this personally. Even if you do not get a response, you have at least put yourself in front of their editor and if you did it right are now on their radar for future coverage. Keep that contact and follow up with another release next time.

Note: *There is a lot to be said for persistence. If you consistently contact an outlet over a period of time, there is a much higher chance that they will eventually cover you. There are so many musicians and bands that it would be impossible for them to cover everyone, but if you can demonstrate that you've been around for a while, are making forward progress, and aren't going away, editors will take notice.*

Present yourself well

During an interview, keep in mind how you want to be perceived by your audience. Especially if it is a video or audio media outlet. Don't be giggling and telling irrelevant stories. Don't cuss a bunch of times, it makes you look stupid even if you are a punk rock band. Tell a linear story of how your band is progressing and what exciting things you have coming up. And the biggest thing: TALK! There is nothing worse than the band who gives a two-word answer to every question. Show people your personality! Be a little bit funny. Be confident but humble; don't put your band above anyone else, thank the people who have helped you, make it look like you are a part of a larger movement that is heading in the right direction (i.e. "The punk scene here in Denver is taking off and really getting attention. We are honored to be a part of it.").

Once the media has aired you or you've been published, **SHARE IT ON YOUR SOCIAL MEDIA ACCOUNTS!** This is the number one way to say 'thank you' for the coverage and get everyone you know to check it out. If you can demonstrate that your social following is active and engaged, you are much more likely to continue getting press coverage. Chapter 4 will discuss the game-changing phenomenon that is social media.

4.

SOCIAL MEDIA PRESENCE

Like it or not, social media is not going away. This is a good thing. There is literally no better way to get the word out about your band than by having consistent, solid social media presence and engaging your audience with thought out, well-placed posts.

Building your social media pages

As a frame of reference, we'll use Facebook since this is the number one platform for showcasing all aspects of your band. We will go over building out a Facebook band page here and then cover how to replicate it across different platforms like Twitter, Instagram, and ReverbNation. Let's start with the basics first. These are things that visitors to your pages are going to look for and notice right off the bat.

Page title

The title of your page should simply be your band or artist name, nothing else. Don't try to be funny or catchy with it. When promoters, media, and other musicians first look at your page it should appear professional. Underneath, it will say Musician/Band. A good idea is to write a post with links to your music, or tickets to an upcoming big show, or whatever it is that you are highlighting at the moment, and 'pin' it to the top of the page. That way, each person viewing the page can easily find that info, and in all likelihood that is why they are there in the first place.

About

Now let's move into the 'About' section. Here, it can be a good place to showcase everything about your band. The most important thing to have on this page is contact information. I cannot tell you how many times I have wanted to check out the phone number or email address for a band and they have nothing listed. Not having a phone number and email provided here is a great way to have promoters, media, and others looking to get ahold of you move on without doing so. It makes you look bad. Yes, they can message your page, but no one wants to do that in a professional setting. Email and phone are always preferred.

Next, list your band members and their instruments. As a journalist, this was the top way I double checked spelling and overall accuracy of members I listed in articles. Links to other social and web pages can be listed here, as well as a short description of your band. The best thing to do is say something simple and easy to reference: "Ska/ Punk from Durango, CO. New EP available on iTunes and Amazon."

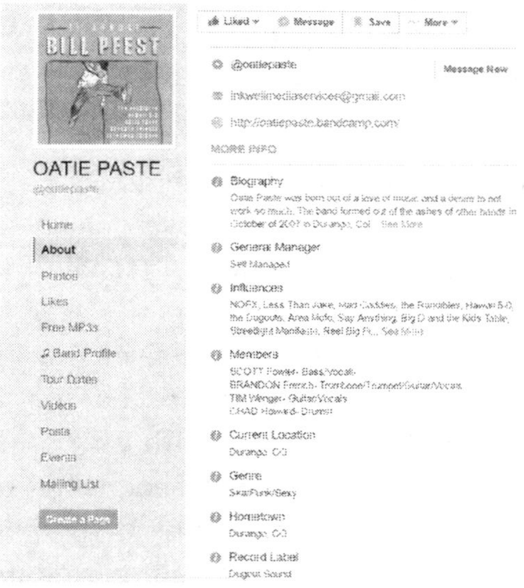

Here you see a very bland, incomplete about page:

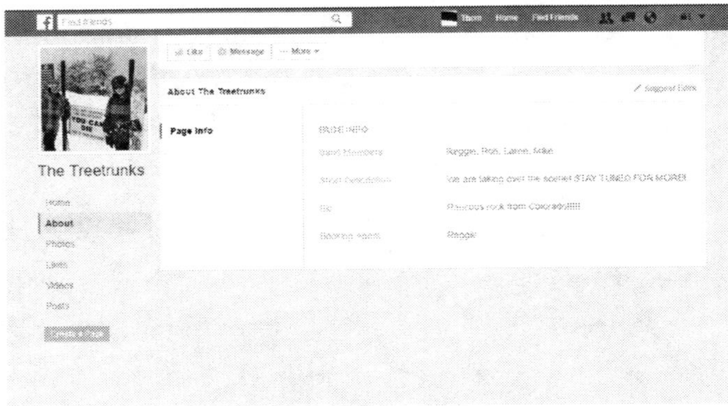

It gives the viewer no frame of reference for who the group is and why they matter. Remember, there are any number of bands out there trying to make an impact. Why are you important? Why should I listen to you?

Bio

Once you have this simple stuff behind you, it is time to put in your band's bio. Do you have one written? Your bio is where you can show some personality while still conveying an accurate story of your group. A great thing to do here is to look at the bio of some of your favorite bands, and other local groups in your genre that are doing well around town. Emulate their bios with your own personal story. Start with a quick paragraph about who you are and what you do. Try to paint a picture in the mind of the reader by setting a scene and moving your group through it.

> *Somewhere in a dark and smoky barroom, a small & dimly lit stage in the corner sits empty but for a chair, microphone, and acoustic guitar. The room is populated with characters, people from all walks of life, sitting over cocktails and dark*

conversations with no clue as to what they are about to witness. As the performer takes the stage, he scans the room to find no one paying much attention and sits down, placing the guitar on his lap and pulling the mic stand in front of him.

Then, move into a paragraph about why you stand out from the rest. Perhaps a funny anecdote or catchphrase, and what someone can expect when watching your show or listening to your music.

With no further warning, the magic happens. John Doe, the man no one noticed walk onto the stage, takes little time silencing the conversations and stealing the attention of each person in the room. Offering a fresh take on the well-worn singer/songwriter circuit, John's music is an amalgam of flavors that hits first with the blues before twisting through rock, adding a dose of hip-hop, and then finally landing listeners on a soft bed of soul. The grittiness and emotion of raw Dylan-esque singing shine bright through his voice, cementing listeners' immediate assumptions that John is a guy that has been around the block. A few songs in you will find yourself, whiskey in hand, drowning your sorrows away with his heart-wrenching songs.

Finally, a quick paragraph about what your group will accomplish in the coming months, and/or what you are working on currently. Also Include previous accomplishments, major names you have shared a stage with and any other reasons why your group is worth checking out.

John is that anomaly that every songwriter wants to be, having traveled the world with a guitar and his notebook – an unabashed performer hurling his brand of articulate, refined lyricism at unsuspecting audiences around the world. He demands the attention of the room from the moment he takes the stage, hypnotizing the crowd with raw talent on the guitar and a lifetime of emotion resting bare on his sleeve. From Denmark to Detroit, Barcelona to Broadway, John Doe is an artist telling the tale of the artist's life.

Apps & photos

There are tons of apps that can be plugged into your band's Facebook page. Only two are worth the time: the 'Tour Dates' app from Bandsintown, where you can easily list all upcoming shows, and a music player, of which there are several to choose from. I recommend ReverbNation's because it will automatically embed each song you have uploaded to your ReverbNation profile.

Photos are key to reaching an audience with your posts. They 'weigh down' the post, which in Facebook's algorithms makes it more important and means it will reach the newsfeed of more people. If you include good, relevant photos in the majority of your posts you will notice more engagement. Additionally, this tactic helps to build up your 'Photos' section, which may be referenced by venues and press to snag a quick picture of your group for a website listing or article.

Replicating across social media platforms

Once you have your Facebook page built, replicate the image on other accounts. Have a consistent name, i.e. don't have your Facebook page titled 'The Treetrunks' and your Twitter account titled 'trtrnksrockdnvr.' Personally, I find it tacky when groups use names that appear conceited or unapproachable, like 'WE ARE THE TREETRUNKS' or

'TREETRUNKS ROCK YOUR FACE.' Use the same bio on each page, and keep the overall image consistent across all accounts. Whenever possible, sync up your accounts using a service such as Hootsuite so that your posts appear consistently across the board.

Posting

Another hint about Facebook is to not over post. Keep your posts meaningful. If you have an announcement, want to do a plug for a show, give a shout out, or share a link to something relevant, by all means, do it. But don't do it five times in two days. Facebook will not show the posts in as many people's feeds if the algorithm determines that you are over-posting or spamming.

Social media etiquette

As tempting as it may be to write a snarky comment about that venue that didn't pay what they said they would or the band that stole your guitar stand, it is imperative that you keep your posts positive. Nobody likes drama queens on Facebook, no matter how justified they may be. Talking shit is a great way to have your page unfollowed, tarnish your reputation, and create a 'what the hell is the deal with those guys?' perception of your band.

Deciding not to play a venue again and perhaps bringing that decision up in conversation with other musicians at a bar or show is one thing, but social media is a whole other ballgame. You can never be quite sure who will see your post and how they will take it. Focus on the positive things your group is doing instead of negative experiences. This will also create an image of your band as 'growing' and 'moving forward.'

Building a following

Social media is an idealized world where people make friends very easily. Impress people. Use your accounts to connect with people around the industry in a positive way. When posting, using hashtags and tag other people relevant to the post such as venues, bands you are playing with, etc. It will help your post reach more people and increase the likelihood of those people sharing the post on their page or retweeting. This is a great way to increase followers and get more interaction with your page.

Boosting posts to a targeted audience is a great way to get in front of new people. Facebook ads allow you to choose pages, interests, and other specifics and then have your post appear in the newsfeeds of people who like those things. For out-of-town gigs, this is highly recommended, especially if it is your first time playing that town. Even putting $5 behind a post can make a big difference in how many people it reaches.

Engaging your audience

- Introduce the band members.
- Ask questions and offer a free song download or sticker for the best answers. Let people know where you will be and encourage them to talk to you.
- Giving shout outs to other bands is a great way to make friends and build relationships. Here in Denver, there is

a long-running ska band called The Dendrites that frequently share songs of other ska bands from around the world on their page- this is a great idea because those bands then are likely to reciprocate or at least start following you (a great way to introduce yourself to larger bands and get on their radar).

- A photo of your band in the van on the way to a show with a caption that reads 'Heading to the Mesa Theatre! See you in a few hours Grand Junction, let's have some beers tonight!" will likely generate a good response from people in Grand Junction that follow your page.
- The last thing is to keep your posts fun! Share a funny photo of your group out back of the club hanging with the other bands after a show.

If you need help creating a bio or have other questions on social media, email me at inkwellmediaservices@gmail.com.

5.

WHERE TO PLAY

There are so many music venues out there. At first, you will have no idea where to start, especially if you live in a big city, and it can certainly be overwhelming. The initial instinct is to play them all, do as many gigs as possible, and hopefully, the right person will be in the crowd one night and sign you to a record deal.

Before confirming with the venue, discussing potential gigs among band members is absolutely essential. Make sure everyone is free and open to the idea, and willing to work hard on promotion. This will minimize the number of times you have to cancel a gig. It also keeps everyone on the same page and in the loop. When deciding whether or not to take a gig, consider the spacing between your booked shows, and also consider whether the lineup fits your style of music and/or if there is an act on the bill that will look good on your group's resume.

Our friends The Treetrunks are having some DIY success. They have put in a multi-year time commitment, built up a following locally and on social media, and brought their brand to new markets through heavy doses of touring, slowly building up a name in different towns. One of the biggest things they have done well is playing the *right* shows. It is not about the quantity of gigs you play.

But how do we find the right gigs, you ask? It takes some research. For a first gig, especially if you are under 21 or haven't played out before, I recommend hitting an open mic night or playing a DIY venue or house party. Feel it out. After you've played out a few times and have your feet under you as far as your stage show goes, you can start to be picky about the gigs you take.

Beware before booking

Something that sparks a fire of rage from just about anyone who has been around the scene a while is *pay-to-play gigs*. As a rule of thumb, you should never open your wallet to play a show. If you are contacted by a promotion company that wants to put your band on their 'Showcase' because they are building an 'eclectic lineup of local up-and-coming artists' and wants you to pre-sell tickets with no cut going back to you, run for the hills. Some production companies set these shows up all over the country and aren't even located in your town or state. It doesn't matter if there are a prize pack and the chance to play in front of a panel of 'industry professionals.' It's a scam. If you have to sell tickets and aren't getting paid, it's a scam for the promotion company to make a bunch of money off young, hungry artists.

Here's how these things work: The scam promotion company will contact a venue that may otherwise be a respectable venue and great place to play, and rent the place out on an off-night like a Sunday or Monday. They handle booking the show. The venue itself has nothing to do with the show other than staffing, and they have already got their cut from the rental fee, so they are hands off (Don't blame the venue, staying in business is hard to do and if they can profit while being open on a Monday night, that's business).

Battles of the bands

Typically, if you are over the age of eighteen, these are to be avoided. They are a route for a venue or promotion company to make money off inexperienced bands that don't know any better, getting them to get everyone they know out to their event to buy tickets and drinks while offering nothing to the majority of the artists.

- If you have not heard of any of the other bands in the 'battle,' say no immediately.
- If the word 'eclectic' is at any point used to describe the lineup (this is true for general booking also), say no immediately.
- My personal opinion is to always avoid battles, even if they aren't worded as such. Something I have seen a lot recently is venues or companies hosting well-known local bands as part of their multi-round battle. If they are doing it, it might be a good chance to share a bill with them and thus be worth it, but do some research. The club or group putting on the battle will likely offer

a decent guarantee and maybe even guaranteed advancement or prizes to a couple well-known bands in the area for them to take part, just to make the contest seem more respectable. This does not change the fact that it is a battle of the bands.

- When considering a battle of the bands, look at the networking opportunities involved. If you can meet larger bands, get in front of their fans, give a cd to the event's high-level sponsors, etc. it might be worth doing. But don't go home crying when you don't win. Typically, these things are rigged.

Finding a venue that suits you

Where are the groups that sound like you playing in town? If you are a punk rock band, it doesn't make much sense to play at the hipster retro bar that mostly books folk rock, even if the place is packed out on most nights.

- If you are a singer/songwriter, taking that late night slot after a five-piece alt rock band doesn't make much sense either. Talent buyers need to fill up their schedules and keep their bars open, so often times (typically on weeknights) you may get offered gigs that aren't ideal for you.
- There is nothing wrong with saying no. In fact, you will be doing everyone including yourself a favor by not playing a show that you don't fit well on.
- When offered a gig, research the other acts on the bill. Ask what time your set will be and how long you will play. Get as many details as you can, and then make a decision after talking with your group.

- Opening for top local bands in your genre is something that should be heavily strived for. Their fans will ideally like your music as well and hopefully become your fans, plus, getting to know them and have them know who you are is a very good thing.
- Booking shows around an event; a birthday, work party, after party for a festival, etc. is typically a strong idea because it will be easier to get people out to see you.

Generally speaking, the shows you play should in some way advance your group. Getting into a venue that you have been wanting to play, even on a Tuesday, making that connection and impressing them can pay off big later.

Dealing with venues that don't suit you

I have worked as a talent buyer for the past few years. It is my job, and that of the other buyer at the club, to keep the place open at least five nights a week by filling each night with a complete lineup of music that will sell tickets and bring people into the venue. As happens often, we will have a slot or two that remain open on an otherwise good looking lineup. In order to fill that slot, we often get on the phone or email with a certain band that we know may not fit the billing perfectly but will bring in a good crowd and is willing to play the closing slot. I'll admit, we use carefully selected language to make that midnight set time sound appealing. Stuff like 'bill you as the headliner' or 'you'll be in front of X Band's crowd if you play right after them' gets thrown around a lot.

Not that these are always a bad thing, but as the person in your band who books the shows it is your responsibility to read between the lines. Is the club actually looking out for you, or are they looking out for themselves? On the other side of the coin, if a band kills it for us in a situation like that, or maybe they worked really hard on a Wednesday night slot that they didn't originally want to play, I am more inclined to throw them a bone the next time and hook them up with direct support for a touring act. There is some give or take here, especially the more you work with a club or promoter and get to know each other.

If the group decides to decline a gig, throw in a brief explanation of why and perhaps offer a couple of upcoming dates that you are available. If you aren't sure if the venue is a good fit for you, leave the upcoming dates out. For example, "Hello Tim, thanks for reaching out!! We are playing Cervantes on 11/20 and cannot play another Denver show that close together. Perhaps a Friday in mid-December could work if you have a bill that we'd fit well on?"

Importance of relationships with venues

It is much better to have a strong working relationship with a few venues that play your style of music regularly than to play one gig at every club in town. Once a talent buyer or promoter gets to know your group and trusts you, bigger and better gigs are in the pipeline with them. The club I book in Denver has been playing live music for over 30 years, and a lot of the long-time musicians in the scene have been gigging there for quite a while. It is not uncommon for musicians to just stop by to say hi while we're working in the office during the day. Many of these groups have become our personal friends and the first people we think of when we need an opener for national bands touring through. They know when we call them for a show, it is because they are the right fit for it and we know that when they recommend a group to put on a bill with them or in place of them if they aren't available, it is worth looking into.

This industry is all about who you know. If there is one thing I can't emphasize enough, it is to build and maintain your list of contacts. Don't burn people. Maybe you played your first show at a certain bar. Your whole crew came out to watch and the bar staff was appreciative of your hard work getting people in the door. You were appreciative of the gig, thanking the bartender at the end of the night. A couple years go by and you haven't returned, but the booking person still has your email address on hand and a note on his calendar that you brought a bunch of people in the door and were easy to work with. Then you get the call when the band you idolize books a show there and they need an opening act.

How often to play

Now that you have a basic understanding of which gigs to take and which gigs to turn down, let's talk about how often to play. As I've discussed before, being able to get people to come watch your show is the single most important element in impressing a venue. A mediocre band that draws really well is going to be playing better shows than an incredibly talented band that only bring their significant others. A key element in drawing a good crowd is to space out your shows. When you first start out, the people that are going to come watch are your friends, family, coworkers, and maybe that guy who lives in your apartment building that is going through a mid-life crisis and wants to feel hip. No matter how happy these people are to support you, they aren't going to come every weekend.

As a young band, a good rule of thumb is one show per month in your hometown. Be impressive on stage. Know the songs well. Make the people want to come to the next show, and hopefully, bring a friend. As you progress and begin to gain a local following and be part of the scene, space out the shows even more. Every six weeks, every quarter. Each gig should be an event that your crowd is excited about and have marked on their calendars and tickets hanging on their fridge. In between local shows, play the next town over (we'll talk about booking out of town in the next chapter). Do a guest spot on a local internet radio station or public access TV using the info you learned in Chapter 3.

6.

DIY TOURING

Touring. The ultimate dream, right? Taking your music and bringing it to the masses, town by town. Living in a van with your best friends and spending each night at a show playing music and shaking hands. It does sound awesome, and if your band gets to a point where you can string together your first small tour, it will undeniably be one of the most challenging, strenuous, crazily fun, and ultimately rewarding experiences of your life. It will be a lot of work, provide very little sleep, and push the relationship between band mates to just about every extreme possible. Think about it this way: you spend every waking moment with the same people. Hopefully, everyone in the group is very tight and close and gets along well. If not, even a small tour of three or four nights can be emotionally straining.

Personally, I've never been in a band at a level where

we were doing full six-week package tours or where we had outside financial or strategic help with our trips. Everything I've done has been 100% DIY, made in-house, underground rock-and-roll touring. So everything I'm going to tell you here comes from experience and learning from mistakes. We never had anyone telling us how to book, how to execute, how to go about anything that had to do with touring. While we did ask some bigger bands for advice when we could, we figured everything out as we went. I'm going to add a personal note here, because ever since I was a teenager going on tour was a dream of mine.

I bought a guitar at fifteen and didn't go on my first tour until I was 23. Even then, I probably wasn't ready for it. We made it through, but definitely made some mistakes along the way that looking back, probably made us look unprofessional in the eyes of the venues and other bands. Being ready to tour is kind of like being ready to have a baby – you're never going to feel perfectly ready. Part of the experience is just doing it and figuring out what works best for your group as you go. My goal here is to help you avoid the mistakes my band made.

The rest of this chapter will be laid out more like a checklist. Before you hit the road, it is important to have certain steps taken care of. While out on tour, it is equally important to keep your shit together. Let's start from the top:

Are you ready to tour?

- Is your band registered as an LLC or another type of business? Do you have tax info figured out?

- Can you draw a decent crowd at home?
- Do you have merch and recorded music? Do not tour without merch! It is the single best way to supplement your income while on the road.
- Do you have a reliable vehicle? What will you do if your van breaks down?
- Plan to buy or rent a trailer.
- How well do you like your bandmates? Are you going to get in a fight and break up in the middle of your tour and make complete asses out of yourselves?
- A lot of touring is similar to gigging at home, as far as being a good band. If you are comfortable, have a strong live show, and understand marketing, try to replicate your action plan on the road. Ask the venues what they are expecting of you. Do you need to mail posters to them? What time is load in for each city? Have you sent your stage plot to the venue? Have they sent you an advance with all of the show info?
- I suggest reaching out to the local bands on the bill asking for a place to crash. Message them on Facebook.

Emotional considerations

One of the biggest mistakes young bands can make is getting it in their head that the band is the only thing that matters in their life and everything else be damned. It is absolutely imperative that you are able to find balance in your personal, work, and band lives in order for this to be a long-term, sustainable thing for you. Bear in mind the following:

- Touring is not a vacation. It's awesome and epic and times you will never forget, but it is also a lot of work. You are never alone for more than a few minutes at a time. You sleep on floors and in the van. You lose money.
- DO NOT BRING YOUR GIRLFRIEND OR BOYFRIEND. Unless she/he understands the point above, and is willing to sell merch and not have their own agenda that they will try to impose on your trip. If someone has a special diet, someone needs to pee every hour, someone gets carsick, these are all factors to think about. When it comes to being on the road on DIY tours, less is more. It is important that each of the band members recognize this.
- Take your significant other out for a nice date before you leave town. Bands are notorious relationship wreckers. Jealousy, lack of commitment, being out late at night and gone frequently, temptation from others at shows, putting the band first and the partner second. These are all struggles that musicians have to deal with in their relationships.
- If you love your partner, make sure they know it. Get their approval for trips and other band happenings that require a lot of your time. Otherwise, you'll end up heartbroken.
- Your partner wants to be the most important thing in your life, and they should be. If you are doing everything that you can to keep your relationship strong, involving your partner and keeping them informed, they should be much more willing and

supportive of your musical endeavors. If they just aren't having it, it might be time to make a decision on whether that relationship or the band is the best thing for you going forward.

Does your financial situation allow you to tour?

Spend some time dealing with your finances before you do any touring of more than a few days. Plan for the future and plan for the worst. I have seen a lot of touring musicians have one of the following work situations:

- They have worked for the same company long enough that they have some flexibility in taking time off frequently. Often they work for a business owned by a family member or close friend and are upfront about their band situation from the get go.
- They work remotely-whether that is in IT, freelance writing or graphic design, web development, whatever. This is the ideal situation for small-time touring musicians because they are their own boss. No approval for time off is needed and often, they won't need the entire tour off work. They can do remote work by having a DIY hotspot on their phone or computer and work during drives. This can be pretty stressful as internet issues will be common, but does provide a good amount of freedom.
- They work in restaurants, bars, or other jobs where getting shifts covered is routine and the schedule isn't always the same week to week. This can provide some flexibility if you end up in the right spot and develop a good relationship with the management/ownership.

I've seen guys just quit their serving job every time they go on tour and find a new one when they get home. I wouldn't recommend this because having income when you get back is absolutely necessary. Otherwise, going out on and coming home from tour is going to turn into a stressful and dreaded situation that will burn you out quickly. Likely, it will end up in you leaving the band in search of more stability, especially if you are in a committed relationship with a girlfriend or boyfriend.

Routing your tour

- How long can you go? How long can everyone get off work? Don't overdo it. When starting out, it is a good idea to do a couple weekend runs, then maybe do a full circle of your state or region, and slowly add a couple new stops each time. Touring should be done in circles, with the circle expanding to add a couple new stops each time.
- How far are you willing to drive in a day? Don't forget that smaller markets like college towns and resort towns can often be great stops on tours. There is not always a necessity to go big city to big city if the drives are more than everyone is comfortable handling. Don't burn yourselves out.
- Understand that when on tour, in order to stay afloat, you need to play every night. Every now and then a show will get canceled or you won't be able to make anything happen, but you should strive to play seven nights a week.
- Again, maybe going for a week at a time, or even

shorter, is best for your band until you get your feet underneath you and some kinks worked out.

- Everyone tours the west coast, maybe you should go somewhere else. Keep it realistic. For The Treetrunks, based out of Denver, there is no need to drive to Seattle or Boston. They should play in Colorado Springs, Albuquerque, Grand Junction, Salt Lake, Kansas, etc. Along with the college and mountain towns in Colorado. The circle thing is important here. Start and end near home whenever possible.
- Target your markets to be places that you can hit once or twice a year, or more. It is pretty much pointless to go somewhere once and never go back. The entire point of a tour is to build a fan base in new markets and that takes time.
- Research promotional tactics for that town. Can you get an interview with a magazine or local college radio station? Use the stuff we talked about in the media chapter. Will you have time to walk the main street and give out handbills? What is the venue expecting from you, if anything?

Organizing tour gigs

- Again, the entire point of touring is to build a fan base in new markets. Start small with bar gigs or all ages DIY rock venues. Check out indieonthemove.com for help.
- Find a local band of a similar genre and offer to do a show trade with them. They host you in their town, you host them in yours. You want to play with local bands

because they will bring a crowd, otherwise, you will likely be playing to an empty room. Do everything you can to find a venue that hosts your style of music. The people and staff in the club will be more likely to both enjoy your band and remember you when you come back.

- Most bars/clubs have booking contact on their websites. A Google search will turn up some spots. Another idea is to find local bands in your genre and look at their show listings to see where they are playing.
- Promote the shows! Hit up local college radio stations about interview/airplay, ask the venue who is in charge of fliers. Get ahold of the flier and buy a Facebook ad targeting that city with a Facebook event, flyer, info on the show, etc. Direct marketing via Facebook can be very effective.
- For DIY clubs that host independent touring acts multiple nights a week, reaching out to them directly can be a good thing. They are all ages and aren't relying on alcohol sales to stay open. Often they are financed by donations and small door charges to cover basic expenses and ran by volunteers from the local music scene. They will be more willing to work with you the first time if you don't have a local draw (which you probably don't).
- Often it is best to contact local bands before blindly contacting a venue, a lot of bar level venues don't care to book out of town bands unless they are playing with locals because no one will come out and they will lose

money opening their doors and paying staff to be there. Locals may already have a show set up and be able to throw you on as an opener.

- Be humble and professional. Don't contact venues blindly through a Facebook message. Create a form letter that can be emailed that looks similar to a press release or EPK: photos, with links to music, a short bio, what you have to offer as regards promotion and draw, the length of the set, maybe even references. The more professional and experienced you come off, the more likely they are to book you.

Sounds great – but how are we going to pay for this trip?

In my experience, local bands are usually pretty cool about money when they are playing with touring bands (at least in the punk world). They get your situation and know that you need to buy gas and food. It's not uncommon (but shouldn't be expected) for a touring band to walk with a larger amount of door revenue than locals. Sometimes, local bands will donate some or all of their take to the touring act. I know that you need to pay for your band's expenses even at home, but this is a GREAT way to make friends with touring bands you play with. It is absolutely appropriate to stay in touch and ask for assistance booking a show in their town. What goes around comes around!

Another idea is to play house parties. If you have friends in a town you'd like to play, perhaps they will throw a party for you and collect donations at the door. This money on top of any merch sales can often be more profitable than playing in bars/clubs that need that are looking out for their own finances more than yours. As a bonus, you've now got your friends promoting your show for you.

While on DIY tours you likely won't profit, but if you book well you can pay your way and attract new fans as you go. This is why it is important to have a proper merchandise setup when touring. Selling a few shirts per night can be huge when it comes to covering daily expenses.

What do to on the road

- Bring a cooler and keep it stocked with sandwich stuff, water, etc. Try to eat healthy, at least most of the time, because you won't be sleeping much and if all you eat is Taco Bell, you'll get worn down and it won't be as fun.
- Try to wait until after your set to party excessively. This is the music business, an industry that loves its partying. People may bring you shots on stage. But if you are a serious musician, getting drunk on stage and playing a sloppy set in a new town is not going to attract anyone to your band.
- Know when the load-in time is, and know who to settle up with after your show. Try to get into town early in case something happens.
- As long as the venue will let you, keep your merch set up from the time doors open until they close, and keep someone at the table. Especially right after your set, go to the merch table and meet people. Shake their hand, hug them, and then sell them your cd.

- ALWAYS have a notebook out to collect emails. Keep the emails organized by town if you can. send out newsletters to these people when you are coming back, when you have a new album out, or new merch, or whatever. Hopefully, they will bring their friends, who then will bring their friends the next time.
- Don't hit on girlfriends/boyfriends of the people in the other bands. Be cool to the other bands because you want to be friends with them. As a musician, being friends with as many other musicians as possible is going to help you so much. You are not a big rock star just because you come from three towns over. Don't be a dick.
- Take a break from the rest of the band before your show. Go on a walk, or go get some food, or do something to get your mind away for a bit. I was on tour with a band on a press assignment once and the guitarist would disappear every day once they finished driving. He would meet the guys at the venue at load in. This seemed a bit extreme to me, but taking any opportunity to have some alone time is a good idea.
- Keep two people awake at all times while driving overnight.
- Be sparing when it comes to hotels and other luxuries. Money is going to be tight. Bring a sleeping bag, pillow and blankets. You'll use the shit out of them. Most of the time you will come home broke. In order to make touring a sustainable part of your life, you need to plan your financial situation to keep afloat without having income while on the road.

- Stop at a laundromat sometimes. You'll be smelly enough as is.
- Remember – enjoy the experience, look to the future, and work hard. But don't get ahead of yourselves. The idea of all of a sudden quitting your job to tour full time, at least to me, proved to be a pipe dream. We constantly let ourselves down because we were never able to get to that point and it ended up hurting our morale greatly. There isn't much money in bar-level gigging for bands without name recognition, certainly not enough to live on. Start small, and be willing to put in a multi-year time commitment to build your band. Keep your head down and work.

There you have it. Some basics for planning, booking, and executing DIY tours.

7.

APPROACHING A BOOKING AGENT OR MANAGER, AND SHOULD YOU REGISTER WITH A PERFORMANCE RIGHTS ORGANIZATION?

The Treetrunks successfully replaced their bassist and are now three years into their career as a band. They have had some ups and downs, some great shows and some lame ones, and have traversed their home state of Colorado numerous times on weekend runs. Plus, they recently did a one-week tour around the southwestern United States booked entirely by themselves. They reached out to local bands and small venues in cities like Albuquerque, Salt Lake City, Flagstaff, and more and strung together six consecutive nights of gigs. Each member was able to take the time off work so that no one came home to the stressful situation of not having any income.

When they got back, they found themselves booking the same clubs, playing with the same local bands, and doing the same stuff over and over (which is a lot of what being in a band is). They started thinking, 'We need a booking agent to put together tours and get us on the best shows locally. That way, we can just focus on the music.' Here are my thoughts on that.

Do you need a manager?

If your group is at a stage where you are playing regularly and you can find a good management company or agency to represent you, that is amazing and should be seriously considered. But here is the deal: only hire a manager if your band is big enough to warrant one. If your hometown shows are well attended, you have a professional recording made, and the group is eyeing a larger chunk of touring in the near future, you are at the level where some outreach can be done.

That said, there are some no-nos. Absolutely do not 'hire' a friend, girlfriend, boyfriend, mom, dad, sister, or brother to 'manage' your band. The whole Mom-ager and Dad-ager concepts are so played out that many in the industry will immediately write your band off as an amateur hour if the manager's last name is the same as the lead singer's.

Talent buyers would much rather deal with the bass player than with her boyfriend, who isn't going to understand anything they are talking about logistically. Plus, having someone as your point of contact who has no experience in the industry is not going to progress your band at all. The whole point of having a manager or booking agent is that they are *more* connected that you are, right?

Making contact with an agency

Let's put The Treetrunks in another situation. Another year passes by, one week tours have turned into two and after working really hard to perfect their stage show, their name is highly respected locally. They even started hosting an annual holiday charity benefit show each December that is becoming a desirable bill for other bands in the scene and generates a good amount of press attention from the weekly alt-newspaper. One day, they check their email account and find a letter from a local agency that represents bands in Denver. The agency puts bands not only on strong local bills but pairs them up with similar groups around the country for show swaps and tour booking. They are interested in meeting with the band and bringing The Treetrunks onto their roster.

This is the best situation for beginning a relationship with management or a booking agency. Ideally, they will reach out to you. If they don't you can send a submission out to them. Some Google research can turn up agencies that may be appropriate and interested in what you have to offer. Target your research to your genre, region, and even city if possible. This should go without saying, but here it is anyway: if submitting to an agency, contest, or anything else, be sure to follow the directions exactly. Don't send more songs than they ask for. Send a bio that is well-written. When filling out forms avoid saying things like "I'm sure you hear this all the time, but. . . "

Befriend bands that are a step ahead of you and emulate what they are doing. Ask them for advice. Likely, they will be happy to tell you how they got picked up by Atomic Music Group and although they won't be able to hook you up, they should be able to explain how it happened.

Meeting with an agency

When meeting with an agency, remember the stuff we have talked about throughout this book. Be professional and present your band as a company and as a brand. Make yourselves as marketable as possible by demonstrating that you have merchandise and music for sale and a strong online presence. Go into the meeting confident about what you've built and how you hope to grow over the next year, two years, five years.

Have one person in the band be the main point of contact for the agency. Be sure they have your EPK and recorded music before the meeting. It will help your chances if you are willing to submit to things they may want you to do like play their annual showcase, attend seminars or networking sessions, or play gigs with the other bands on the roster frequently. Be ready to part with 20% of any revenue your band earns if you make the decision to work with an agency or manager.

Perhaps the most important thing is to do what feels right. If someone approaches you, or you find a company online, and it seems like the perfect fit, proceed confidently. Don't beat yourself up if it doesn't work out. There are a ton of scams out there (just check the musician's section on Craigslist in any major city). It is better to represent yourself and keep going on your path than to work with someone who is trying to take advantage of you or has no idea what they are doing. The beauty of being a musician these days is that nearly everything can be done independently. Many well-established bands represent themselves.

Should we register with a Performance Rights Organization?

The main function of Performance Rights Organizations (PROs) are responsible for collecting royalties on their members' copyrighted work. Nearly all major artists use one to handle royalty collections from radio stations, television networks, venues, and public outlets that use copyrighted music in their business. For example, the song used in a car commercial is likely copyrighted by the artist or their label. The PRO comes in to collect money for the use of that work, if a separate contract has not been put in place. The PROs distribute funds in the form of royalty checks.

In the US, the major performance rights organizations are ASCAP, BMI, and SESAC. In Canada, many artists use SOCAN. PROs are a great way to ensure you get paid for your music if it is licensed for use outside of your performances and recordings. ASCAP charges $50 per submission of copyrighted material, while BMI is free to join for songwriters and $150 for publishers. SESAC requires an invite to join.

Whether or not you should sign up with one depends on how seriously your group plans to push your recorded music. I absolutely think registering with a PRO is a good idea for groups planning to tour, have music distributed digitally and physically (although PROs don't always collect royalties for every digital play or sync), and work towards any type of licensing for commercial use. Likely, there won't be a ton of royalty money coming your way but a few bucks here and there never hurts. Signing up is easy to do at ASCAP or BMI's website.

As far as picking an organization, BMI is more straightforward for newer artists. You will not need to have a publishing company collect your royalties for you from BMI and they pay royalties quarterly. ASCAP does require a publishing company, but artists can sign up with a company like Songtrust to handle that part if they wish. It's pretty easy to do.

In short, independent musicians should register with a performance rights organization. It is an easy way to ensure you will get paid for use of your work.

8.

YOUR IMAGE AND WHY YOU NEED TO CONSISTENTLY RELEASE MUSIC

Let's do an exercise here. Think about your favorite artists. Make a list of your three favorite acts that are currently active and working. Then, make a list of the top three bands or artists in your local music scene right now. How frequently do you hear from each of them on social media? Very regularly, I'd venture to guess.

We talked quite a bit about social media back in Chapter 4, and I'm going to spend some time elaborating on it here while tying it into why your group needs to release music consistently.

Some things change, some stay the same

Before the days of the internet, (oh, so long ago!) bands released full-length albums every year or two, did a tour to promote the album, periodically promoting songs from the album as singles to keep radio play up and entice new buyers and fans. Back then, record labels had more money to back artists so bands could concentrate on recording. At the time, album sales made up a solid chunk of a musician's income, so it was absolutely imperative both socially and financially to have a new song drop on a regular basis.

Even though an album might only happen every two or three years, there were multiple 'releases' of songs from that album. Why? The answer is simple; to remain relevant and top-of-mind. Consistent releasing of music keeps your name in people's head, keeps a fresh track in their ear, and makes it seem like the group is constantly working and moving forward. Despite the fact that the full-length album is less common for young bands these days, the concept of single releases and/or videos still remains popular.

I interviewed a young band at Riot Fest in 2013. After "hustling the fuck out of LA," to put their self-made success into their own words, the band was asked to join one of punk rock's biggest names on a summer tour, concluding at the Colorado stop of Riot Fest. I asked them what the single most important factor in their success was. Their answer? Giving away their music for free. Allowing free downloads increased the people owning and listening to their music, sharing it with friends, and coming to their shows. Likely, you have no record deal or financial backing from someone outside the band. Also, you are probably not selling a ton of music. It's in your best interest to have your songs heard by the largest audience possible.

Moving forward

Remember what I discussed earlier about positive posting on social media? Show people you're moving forward, make friends, create a strong vibe around your group, etc.? Releasing music regularly is perhaps the best way to do just that. It will embed a sense that your group is moving forward, progressing and growing, and is on the track to success (which you are). This makes people more likely to support you, to share your posts, and to interact regularly with the group. Everyone wants to be the next big thing, and if they can't be it themselves, they want to associate with it.

To keep this growth happening and the shows popping, consistent releasing of music is key. Look back at the lists you made at the beginning of this chapter. Look at the social media profiles of those artists. Do they have a single out, or a new EP, music video, etc.? Something to keep their audience engaged? If they are currently active and working hard, odds are the answer is yes.

Releasing songs

Come up with a schedule for releasing songs. Even if you record them all at once, consider releasing the songs one by one along with a lyric video or new piece of merchandise to go along with it. Then, after a few songs are out, drop the EP or album and throw a huge party at your favorite venue to celebrate. Releasing songs on a monthly basis, or six-week basis, or hell, even every other week for newer bands, keeps your audience engaged and you will notice an increase in the amount of interaction you'll get through your social pages. Hopefully, this will translate into increased attendance at shows.

When a song release happens, be prepared to spend some time and money promoting it. Reference what your favorite bands are writing in their release posts. Write up a similar post and share the song via YouTube. Sponsor the post and target that sponsorship to fans of your genre's most successful bands, in addition to the local music media in your town (see Chapter 4). Write a press release for each song drop, and blast it out to appropriate music blogs and media (see Chapter 3). If you can, work with a blog or local media outlet to premiere the song. They may embed the YouTube video or SoundCloud stream into a post on their website. Great way to get exposure for your track.

Have you thought about making a music video? In the age of GoPro, smartphones, and YouTube, putting together a decent music video is not hard to do. It doesn't have to be fancy. If you can afford to hire a professional to shoot a video, do it. Research a local filmmaker or someone who has made music videos for other groups in your city. But that isn't a necessity. Have a friend film your group playing the song at practice, at a show or house party, and include some footage of the crew hanging out or doing an activity together. Use a simple editing studio like GoPro Studio and put together a video where the shot changes every few seconds. Or, even simpler, just make a creative lyric video that displays the lyrics as they appear in the song. Some simple internet research can teach you how to put together a lyric video.

Benefits of consistently releasing

The public image and perception of your band will benefit immensely from well-promoted song releases and videos. Consistent releasing of music gives promoters, talent buyers, and potential fans in your market and beyond a great first impression of you. If they head to your Facebook page and see these type of posts, they are going to view you in a professional manner immediately. You'll be taken seriously right from the get-go.

9.

COPYRIGHTING AND MUSIC LICENSING

It seems so easy to curse the music business these days. Fans aren't spending the money on music that they used to, which has greatly reduced the amount of income recording artists pull in off their songs. As a result, many bands are forced to spend much more time touring than ever before as a way to bring in revenue.

If your group is at the point where you have professionally recorded music, you are probably looking to get it into the hands of as many people as possible. If you aren't, you should be. Please, don't sit around trying to sell your album for $15 and then wonder why no one is buying it. It is absolutely imperative that people have access to your songs. At the very least, the general public should have the ability to stream them whenever they desire.

Another way artists are bringing in royalties, and gaining great exposure through their music, is through licensing agreements with radio, television programs and commercials, film, or any other medium that incorporates a soundtrack into their business model. In order to license your music, you must copyright it first. In this chapter, we'll go over how to legally copyright your music and the basic protocols of music licensing agreements. We're going to get into some legal talk here, but don't worry, the terms are very basic and you'll impress people with this knowledge. Big thanks to my lawyer friend Will Kilduff, Esq. (Ret.) for his assistance with this chapter.

What is copyright?

At its core, a copyright is a legal right that grants the creator of a piece of intellectual property (like a song) the exclusive right to use it, market it, and distribute it. Songs are limited in their copyright by things such as the Fair Use policy. This policy allows limited use of copyrighted material without permission from the owner or the payment of royalties. In the music world, this means that public domains can use part of the song for educational or non-profit means. There is a rumor widely circulated that fair use grants permission to use up to 30 seconds of a song for any purpose. This is completely bogus. Even sampling someone else's song in one of your songs can be challenged these days, so it is always better to ask for permission if you wish to sample someone's music.

This won't affect most bands. But what you do need to know is how to copyright your work and, once it is copyrighted, how to grant someone else permission to use it. In most cases, the duration of a copyright spans the creator's life plus 50 to 100 years.

The process is quite simple. To register a copyright, head to this address: http://copyrightregistry-online-form.com/ (or search 'Register a Copyright' on Google if you can't click the hyperlink).

What copyrighting covers

Once you have copyrighted your music, you generally obtain these rights:

- to produce copies or reproductions of the work and then sell them
- to import, export, upload, and give permission to download the work
- to create derivative works by reworking your songs, or sample the songs in future creations
- to perform or display the work in public and for profit
- to sell or cede the right to others
- to transmit or display by radio or video

So, you can basically do as you choose with your music as long as you own the copyright. Before streaming, downloading, and the internet, in general, came along, artists would often sign the right to their music over to their record label. One of the benefits of being a DIY musician in this day and age is that you probably won't have to worry about that. Just about everything a record label can do for you can be done by yourself or by a management team, without giving up ownership of your music.

On the other hand, copyright will not cover:

- Names of products
- Names of businesses, organizations, or groups. This is tricky. You may have heard about bands receiving cease and desist letters from other bands with the same name. If this happens to you and you are not very far along, I recommend tagging on an additional word or digits to your name or changing it completely. Otherwise, consult a lawyer.
- Titles of works, i.e. a song title- many songs share the same name as other songs. Don't worry about naming your song a certain way for fear that another song has already been called that.

There are additional exceptions to what copyrights will and will not cover. Often, these are determined on a case by case basis if a legal proceeding ends up happening. Generally, you will want to register each piece of work you create as a copyright. If your band is releasing an album or EP, register it as one, but if you release songs one at a time that will not be part of a larger collection, you may want to register them individually, although this costs more money and takes more time.

What about the poor man's copyright, you ask?

The poor man's copyright entails the creator of a work mailing a copy of that work to him or herself in the mail, with the postage date serving as the registration date to prove that the work was created on or before that date. My band did this for our first album. Because we've never been challenged on anything regarding it, it has worked fine, but I can no longer recommend doing this. Although it can offer some solid defense in court, the United States Copyright Office does not recognize the practice as an official copyright. Publishing the music online is about as effective as mailing a copy to yourself because the date of upload can be proven in court, although that still does not classify as an official copyright. If you plan to license your music or distribute it in any way, take the time to copyright the work legally and avoid any headaches down the road.

Licensing

Licensing your music can be one of the best ways to expose yourselves to a much wider audience and also to earn income of your songs. Of course, this is assuming your music is top notch and recorded on professional equipment. When dealing with licensing, there are a number of third party Publishing Companies that can represent you and work on your behalf.

These companies work with producers of media that need recorded music to earn placements for their clients. I highly recommend working with a licensing company if you can. Some are very choosy about who they work with and some are not as effective as others, but the biggest plus for the artist is that these companies know the process from start to finish.

Types of license

The most commonly used license is a Synchronization Agreement, which grants the licensee permission to sync music with some kind of visual outlet such as a commercial or video game. Often, though, when licensing music to a media producer such as someone creating a television commercial, movie, or show, a 'master use license' will be in order. This agreement grants someone permission to use the copyrighted material in a visual work. Here is a great PDF download of a master use license- http://www.newmandecoster.com/pdf/masteruse.pdf. In special situations, a licensee may pay an annual fee for a blanket license to use a specified catalog of songs in their media creations. In other situations, a Masters License may be used by the person who owns the recording and the person who wishes to use the material. But typically, a sync license for a specific piece of music is used. The artist will always be paid a set amount for use of their song, ranging anywhere from a few pennies to thousands of dollars.

How to get a licensing agreement

Now that you know how license arrangements work, of course, you are going to want to know "How the hell do I get my song into these situations?" Well, this can be tough. The first and most important factor is to have top quality recordings. It certainly doesn't hurt your cause if you play a style of music that is popular in the mainstream, or that is frequently found in TV commercials and movies. Unfortunately for metal heads, most producers of TV commercials aren't looking to use a death metal song to advertise a product.

If you are recording an album, talk with the engineers at the studio where you record and see if they have any recommendations for outlets that may want to use your music. It is in their best interest as well as yours to have your music receive as much publicity as possible, so odds are if they have any connections or ideas they will be willing to share.

Many publishing companies will accept submissions and may even be willing to meet with you. Be sure to put your best foot forward in these circumstances. Send your best song, after it is completely done with mixing and mastering along with a flawless electronic press kit, or follow their specific instructions for submissions. Don't send more than they ask for. Keep any email contact brief and to the point. It is a good idea to have someone who is a professional writer or PR person compose a couple of paragraphs for you if no one in the band is confident in their writing abilities. Having had songs played on local college radio or internet stations is a plus and should be mentioned. Having a strong online presence with a good number of followers, solid lineup of gigs, and an overall presence that demonstrates you have your ducks in a row is crucial in getting signed up by these companies.

10.

PROBLEMS WITHIN THE BAND

What happens when something goes wrong?

Let's go through a scenario here. Our example band, The Treetrunks, have been together for two years now. They got their feet wet playing weeknight gigs at small venues around town, worked hard to get their friends and family out to watch their shows, and eventually started getting better gigs. Weekends became the norm. The band has a few weekend road trips under their belt and because they were on top of promo and acted real professional when they played in other towns, have built a good relationship with the venues. They've even gotten the call to open for a couple of mid-level nationals at a 500-capacity theater in their hometown, and the guys are *still* best friends.

But the bass player and his girlfriend just got pregnant. Oh shit. Now, his expenses are about to go through the roof while his availability goes into the cellar. He shows up to practice and is incredibly stressed out, and after some prodding from the other guys, finally admits that he is going to have to leave the band. The rest of the group is stunned. Everything seemed to be progressing and they were finally starting to gain some momentum. Now the band has to find a new bassist.

Band members may come and go, and this is common. It is extremely rare to see a band retain the same lineup over a career spanning multiple years. Things come up; significant others, jobs, financial situations, family, all of these things can and should take priority over a band that is not generating a livable revenue. In the first paragraph of this chapter, I noted that the bass player of The Treetrunks was leaving after two years. This timeframe was significant.

Most bands are not going to last more than two years. Some burn out after only six months. Finding the right people with the right passion and who are all at the right point of their lives to dedicate significant time and sacrifice to make a band work long term is a very hard thing to do. This is especially true when money comes into play. Finding a job to support you financially while you take time off to travel, record, and play shows is not an easy task. To add to the struggle, even bands who tour frequently and maybe even have a small record label helping with marketing or distribution are still not making any profit. The members work jobs or run their own business when they aren't on the road.

Dealing with a break-up

Continuing with the above example, the bass player holds an equal share in the company, is he willing to give up his share? If the band has anything under copyright, he will still likely be entitled to any royalties that the band incurs as long as the agreement granted him partial ownership of the music. New papers are going to need to be drawn up dictating that any intellectual property created after the agreed upon date of departure from the member, or revenue generated after the agreed upon date of departure, will not include the departing member unless utilizing intellectual property that he is a part of. This is easy enough to do, and in most cases, the departing member should happily agree to sign on to this.

How is the group going to go about replacing this person? Craigslist can be a good way to source people to audition for the spot if no one in the group knows of someone. I highly recommend hiring someone with experience equal to what the rest of the band has, and preferably someone who will be willing to not be included as a member of the legal company until after a set trial period. This will give the group and the new member a chance to part ways if it doesn't work out. Once the group has settled on the right person, he or she can be added as a shareholder or partial owner of the business. You'll want to find someone that can become a close friend, not just someone who is an incredible musician.

Band burn-out

The truth is that as a band progresses, it becomes increasingly hard to balance it with day to day life. Significant others get jealous or feel underappreciated. Many relationships, including one multi-year relationship in my own life, have ended because that person feels second in importance compared to the band. Jobs don't work out as the employer gets tired of not being prioritized. Bills add up. It is a very stressful truth that any seasoned musician can relate to. In the end, many musicians just don't want to deal with the pressure anymore and decide to pull the plug. Sometimes it is a personal decision, other times it is forced by something like having a kid or a job opportunity that can't be passed up.

The number one thing that burns bands out, and I have been through this myself, is what I call 'chasing the carrot syndrome.' We grow up watching our favorite bands shred it on stage, rocking out to their songs in the car, and staring at them from the floor at shows. All the while thinking about how awesome it would be to be the one up there, sharing your passion with the world, making it happen. Living the dream of spending your nights on the stage and days in the van. Bills paid by selling merch and the royalty check waiting for you in the mailbox when you get home from tour. While everyone you know is at work, you are headed to the next gig or laying down tracks at the studio. Every person that you've ever crushed on would have no choice but to recognize your greatness.

So you start a band. Time passes and you keep feeling like

you're so close. So close to being able to quit your job and tour. So close to getting that huge offer to do a run of shows with your idols and convert their fans to yours.

Living with reality

What no one ever tells you (until now) is that it is not going to happen. I'll come right out and say it. You are not going to make a living as a musician, at least not for the rest of your life. Most independent bands, the ones that tour all year and drop an EP each season, have absolutely zero money. Their lives in the present may seem great. They are living their dream and blasting it all over social media.

But eventually, each member is going to want something more. When you've been living broke for ten years trying to make your dream happen, watching girlfriends come and go, and constantly moving your stuff from apartment to apartment, having some steadiness in your life starts to sound really good. A friend once told me that 'You can't just Jack Kerouac around anymore.' He was talking about bumming around and working temp jobs forever until you finally make it as a writer. But there is a lot of truth to the statement for musicians as well.

Everyone needs to feel valuable and to do that, they need to make a living. If you're touring enough that you don't need an apartment right now, what happens when you have to come home? What happens when every single person you know from high school and college are married with kids and you are still out till 3 AM every night? Now, people love to go on rants about how memories are more important than money. They are absolutely correct. But that doesn't change the fact that every single person needs to get by, somehow, someway. If all of your memories end up with you having to call your parents or best friend to borrow money so that you can get by for another week, your self-confidence (and your relationships) are going to hit the floor.

How to prolong the dream

The musician's life is incredibly appealing on the outside. If you do it right, it is the same way on the inside, but therein lies the problem – most bands don't do it right. Where is that line in the sand? How do you know if *you* are doing it right? If you follow the steps in this book and, I'll repeat it again, are willing to put in a time commitment spanning several years, you will be on the right track. But if you expect to be there in six months, or even two years, there is going to be a hard, painful, and often sudden crash into the burn out wall. It can be a slow realization that the lifestyle you see portrayed on social media and at shows is an incredibly hard thing to achieve. So many bands break up because of this realization. It can be hard to accept. The important thing to remember is that it is not necessarily a sign of your band any more than it is a sign of the times.

In the music business, there is a silver lining. There are plenty of jobs that revolve around the industry and many that will even support your band in one way or another. After you've been around the block as a musician, no matter how far you are able to take it, use your experiences and your contacts to leverage the next step. Get a job at a venue. Learn how to run a soundboard or record music.

Buy a screen printing setup. As I mentioned before, there is also the concept of working for yourself or in a family business that is cool with taking frequent time off (there are numerous books to get you on the path to doing this). If you can pull this off, you'll have a much better chance at keeping the 'rock star' dream alive for as long as possible. Starting a band was an entrepreneurial venture – what have you learned that you can parlay into a career step that allows you to at least work within the industry you love?

Network!

I can never emphasize this enough – maintain your contacts! Meet as many people as you can. Get their number. Friend them on Facebook. Be good to them. You never know how they may be able to help you or who they can plug you into down the line. That promoter that you've played for might be able to recommend you to another promoter, but he might also be able to plug you into a talent buying job at the venue he works with. Show up to events. Accept invites. I got my job as an editor at a music magazine largely because I showed up to an event that I knew the publisher would be at. I made a point of shaking his hand. I impressed him with my persistence and was willing to contribute articles for a while to show him what I could do. Basically, I networked my way to an awesome job. It all started because I had experience playing and touring. Then, I got a job as a talent buyer at a 500-cap room because over the course of the next few years the magazine did a number of events at that club. I befriended their staff and in particular, was friendly with the head talent buyer.

11.

FINAL THOUGHTS

Follow your passions. People always say that but few actually live it. I see no reason why a person, given the ability to do so, should not spend as much time as possible working toward the things that give them the most joy. For me, and I'm guessing you too since you've bought this book, playing music is one of those passions. Getting onstage and rocking out with my best friends, watching people dance and smile and have a great time, is a feeling unparalleled by any drug I've ever taken. Going on my first out-of-state tour marked the fulfillment of a life ambition I set for myself as a teenager.

My wife will be the first to tell you I am a sentimental guy. I definitely had tears of joy in my eyes as I drove through the desert with my band in the middle of the night on that tour, catapulting south on I-15 on our way from a show in Salt Lake City to our next stop in Prescott, AZ.

Sleeping in sleeping bags outside the van on the side of a dirt road in the middle of nowhere, or tucked together like Lincoln Logs in the living room of some random stranger's apartment might sound terrible to most people, but in a musician's reality, it is oh-so-glamorous. The highs I've felt from playing a great show or making new friends on the road are life experiences I would not trade for anything. I'll admit, now that I haven't been gigging as much over the last few years, I get jealous when I see friends posting on Facebook about their experiences, typically accompanying a photo of their band with mile-wide smiles on their faces. Being in a band is fucking awesome.

To me, the work that goes into it is enjoyable, inspiring, and motivating. I remember so many nights as a teenager, fighting my way through the mosh pit up to the front of the crowd at packed shows and standing up against the divider. Staring up at the guys onstage, I saw everything I ever wanted out of life. I had no idea what it took to get there, I just knew I wanted it so badly that I would do anything.

It never turned into a full-time career like I thought it would. This, I must confess, is the biggest piece of advice I can offer young bands: don't become a victim of the 'chasing the carrot' syndrome. Realize early on that growing a band is a multi-year commitment that requires everyone in the group to be on-board 100%. Additionally, it requires each member of the band figuring out how to take this activity that takes a great deal of time, a moderate amount of financial investment, and a whole lot of uncertainty, and work it into their personal lives.

In order to make your band work long term, it is important to think big picture and incorporate your band's goals into your long-term personal planning. It is going to be an emotional rollercoaster. Some days you'll be on top of the world, others you'll be convinced you are wasting your time. You'll often feel like you are falling behind in life as you watch friends get married, have kids, make good salaries, and settle down. But remember to follow your passion. Stick with it. Grow your personal life as well, not everything has to be about the band. If you do these things and stay on track, you'll begin to see results trickle in. Then one day you'll find yourself standing on stage, looking out into the audience as you rip through your best song, and you'll see a kid fight his way to the front of the crowd just for the chance to look up at you.

RESOURCES FOR MUSICIANS

Indie on the Move: www.indieonthemove.com

Bandsintown: https://www.bandsintown.com/facebook

Reverbnation: https://www.reverbnation.com/

Copyright: http://copyrightregistry-online-form.com/

LyricHouse: http://lyrichouseco.com/

Master Use License: http://www.newmandecoster.com/pdf/masteruse.pdf

Sampling music: http://blog.mediamusicnow.co.uk/2009/04/18/fair-use-music-copyright/

BMI: http://www.bmi.com/creators/#careertools

ASCAP: https://www.ascap.com/licensing

SESAC: https://www.sesac.com/WritersPublishers/WritersPublishers.aspx

SOCAN: http://www.socan.ca/licensees

Independent Music in the Internet Age, by William P. Kilduff, Esq. (Ret.)

SAMPLE BAND PARTNERSHIP AGREEMENT

Introduction:

This Band Partnership Agreement is made between the following individuals (collectively referred to as “Band Partners”):

This agreement will be in effect as of the date of the final signature at the bottom of the document (“Effective Date”). The Band Partners agree as follows:

The Band Partnership:

The Band Partnership establishes themselves as a general partnership to be known as (Band Name) ________________

Under the laws of (State/Country/Region) ____________

For the purposes of musical and related entertainment activities. The Band Partnership will commence on the Effective Date and will continue until it is ended according to this Agreement. The principal place of business of the Band Partnership will be at (Address)

Band Partner Services:

In order to fulfill the Band Partnership purposes, each Band Partner will contribute musical entertainment services to the Band Partnership. Such contributions include, but are not limited to:

- serving as a recording artist with respect to sound recordings
- serving as a musical performer in all media and on the live state
- relating merchandising rights using logo, name, and other identifiers to the Band Partnership

Non-Band Partnership Activities:

Each Band Partner is permitted to engage in one or more businesses, including other musical entertainment efforts, but only to the extent that such activities do not directly interfere with the business and obligations of the Band Partnership. Neither the Band Partnership nor any other Band Partner will have any right to any income by a Band Partner from any non-Band Partnership activities.

Name and Logo:

The Band Partnership will do business under the name(s)

As an assumed name and as its trademark and service mark.

The Band Partnership also uses the following logo:

Insert Band
Logo Here

Domains and web addresses operated by the Band Partnership: www.band-website.com

Warranties:

Each Band Partner warrants that he or she:

- is free to enter into this Agreement
- is under no restriction that will interfere with this Agreement
- has not done nor will do an act that may hurt the Band Partnership
- will not sell or transfer any interest in the Band Partnership without the prior written consent of the other Band Partners
- will refrain from activities that could prohibit him or her from performing

Each Band Partner indemnifies each other from all claims that may arise from any breach of these warranties.

Profits and Losses:

The Band Partnership will share in all of the Net Profits, losses, rights, and obligations of the Band Partnership at agreed upon levels during each accounting year, assuming that the Band Partner is still under obligation of this Agreement.

"Net Profits" will mean all payments, (with the inclusion or exclusion of) publishing, licensing, and synchronization rights, that are paid to the Band Partnership or to any Band Partner as a result of Band Partnership activities, after deduction of Band Partnership expenses to include rent, travel, hospitality, accounting and legal fees, other reasonable expenses as agreed upon by Band Partnership).

The Net Profits will be distributed in cash to the Band Partners.

If a Band Partner is expelled or withdraws from Agreement, he or she retains earned songwriting and publishing rights for songs released prior to the partner leaving, but terminates rights to other forms of Band Partnership income.

Division of Publishing Revenue:

Revenue from the Band Partnership Publishing Company, if such publishing company has been created, will be distributed as follows:

- Songwriting Revenue shall be split according to the

songwriting split paperwork signed for each song upon its contract with a licensing/publishing company.

- Publishing Revenue shall be split equally among all members of the band. Only current band members shall receive publishing revenue. When a Band Partner leaves the Partnership, his or her share of songwriting revenue no longer includes publishing income but retains Songwriting Revenue as legally documented for each song.

Publishing Administration:

The Band Partnership or Band Partnership Publishing Company will have the worldwide, exclusive right to:

- administer and control to he copyright ownership to the Recorded Compositions
- designate all persons to administer the copurights to the Recorded Compositions
- enter into agreements to co-publish, sub-publish, or otherwise deal with the copyrights in the Recorded Compositions.

In the event that one of the Band Partners leaves the Band Partnership , the control of the jointly owned copyrights will vest exclusively in the remaining Band Partners for the term of this Band Partnership. The Leaving Member's interest in the Band Partnership will extend only to those Recorded Compositions which were commercially released for sale during the Leaving Member's period as a Band Partner. Any payments and accountings due Leaving Member will be made annually.

Meetings and Voting:

Each Band Partner has the right to participate in the business of the Band Partnership. Meetings of the Band Partners can be called by any member of the Band Partnership on reasonable notice. Voting will occur as follows (here, check whether the decision is determined by a unanimous or majority vote):

Unanimous Majority:

(These are things to discuss and include in the agreement in order to ensure everyone is on the same page- specifically, whether action on these items requires consent from every member. In the agreement this sample was built from, these were the items that needed a 'unanimous majority' for the action to be taken.)

Expelling a Band Member (unanimous except for party to be expelled)

Admission of a new Band Partner

Entering Into Agreements that binds the Band Partnership for more than one year

Any expenditure in excess of $1000

Incurring obligation to borrow or lend money

Selling, leasing, or transferring Band Partnership Property

Entering into contracts that take less than one year to complete

Amendment of this Agreement

Dissolving the Band Partnership

If one Band Partner is to have extra voting power or the ability to override decisions, state that member here

Books of Account and Records:

The books of the Band Partnership and all other documents relating to the Band Partnership will be maintained at its principal place of business, or online at this address:

The fiscal year of the Band Partnership ends on December 31.

Distribution of Band Assets after Termination:

- **Income and Debts:** After termination of the Band Partnership, any income that is owed to the Band Partnership will be collected and used first to pay off Band Partnership debts (if any) within or outside of the Partnership, as they relate to the Partnership. Any remaining money will be distributed among the members in accordance with their voting power or ownership in the company.
- **Band Property:** Any property owned or controlled by the Band Partnership will be sold or evaluated and distributed in accordance to each member's voting power or ownership in the company.
- **Royalties and Future Income:** If, at the time of termination, the Band is entitled to royalties or owns

property that is generating income or royalties, the Band Partnership will vote to either establish an administrative trust or designate an individual such as an accountant to collect and distribute the royalties on an ongoing basis to the Band Partners according to their respective interests.

Addition of a new Band Partner:

Each new Band Partner must agree to be bound by all of the provisions in this Agreement. A new Band Partner has no rights to Band Partnership property or assets existing at the time of admission or in any of the proceeds derived from Existing Property (assets existing at the time of admission).

Leaving Members:

A Band Partner may leave the Partnership voluntarily. A Band Partner who resigns must give 60 days prior notice. A leaving member is entitled to their share of assets, royalties, or incomes generated during their time in the Band Partnership as described in this Agreement.

Band Partnership Bank Account:

A bank account may be opened by the Band Partners. This account will be used for business pertaining to the Band Partnership.

Mediation, Arbitration:

If a dispute arises under this Agreement, the parties agree to first try to resolve the dispute among themselves. If this cannot happen, a mutually agreed upon mediator will assist in resolving the dispute, to include a lawyer if necessary. Any costs and fees other than attorney fees will be shared equally by all parties. If it is impossible to arrive at a mutually satisfactory solution within a reasonable time, the parties agree to submit the dispute to binding arbitration pursuant to the Commercial Arbitration Rules of the American Arbitration Association.

Any decision or award as a result of any arbitration proceeding will include the assessment of costs, expenses, and reasonable attorney's fees and a written decision by the arbitrators.

MY SIGNATURE BELOW INDICATES THAT I HAVE READ AND UNDERSTOOD THIS AGREEMENT AND HAVE BEEN ADVISED OF MY RIGHT TO SEEK INDEPENDENT LEGAL REPRESENTATION REGARDING THIS AGREEMENT:

Full Name: ______________________________

Signature: ______________________________

Date: _______________

SAMPLE PRESS CONTACT EMAIL

From: John Smith <john@email.com>

To: Colorado Music Buzz <press@cmbzz.com>

Subject: FOR IMMEDIATE RELEASE: The Treetrunks Drop New Single, Headline Herman's Hideaway Aug. 5

Denver, Colorado alt-rockers The Treetrunks are bringing their catchy blend of pop-rock and alternative to Herman's Hideaway on Friday, August 5. The music video for the band's newest single "Climbing High" is out NOW – see link in below press release.

I'd love to set up an album review or interview with Colorado Music Buzz! As a Denver band, the group has a lot to say about the local scene and their place in it. Let me know if you are interested and how you'd like to proceed. An advance media copy of their upcoming album is attached for your review.

Best,

Tim Wenger
The Treetrunks

<Attachment: Treetrunks Press Release>

SAMPLE PRESS RELEASE

The Treetrunks Working With Big Name Producer, Dropping Album May 19

Denver, CO – Denver-based alt rock band The Treetrunks will be celebrating the release of their new album with three shows in Colorado coupled with record store and radio appearances around the state from May 19-22. These dates mark the beginning of a nearly three month long national tour- catch details and updates here.

But this isn't just another band releasing another album. The band worked with legendary producer xxxxxxxxxx in the studio for three months, painstakingly working the songs to perfection. "I don't think they could sound any better," says front man John Doe. The band performed their first ever sold out theatre show this spring in Colorado Springs. "It was a huge move for us... the reaction from the crowd was amazing and we could all feel the energy in the room," says Doe.

The band is excited to share their new music, and happy to be in Colorado for its release. The new album will be dropped at midnight on 5/19, just after their headlining set at the Marquis Theatre in Denver, and will be available on Spotify, iTunes and Amazon Music. Physical CDs will be available for advanced purchase at the concert.

The album reveals the band's shift towards a new direction, with the writing process including collaboration with artists across many genres. And through the songwriting the band shows no signs of holding back, going full speed ahead with message-driven, anthemic alternative rock. Check out the single premier and review by PopMatters, "BAND BIO HERE"

Colorado dates:

May 19- Marquis Theatre, Denver

May 20- The Black Sheep, Colorado Springs

May 21- Victoria Tavern, Salida

The band is available for interviews and other press inquiries.

Media Contact: John Johnson, 555-555-5555 or xxxxxxx@gmail.com

ABOUT THE AUTHOR

Tim Wenger is a Denver-based journalist and music biz aficionado reporting for multiple publications since 2010. He produces media content across the music, travel, and winter sports platforms, and handles talent booking and oversight for music venues and festivals.

After pursuing a BA in English/Communications from Fort Lewis College in Durango, Tim jumped in a Ford Econoline for a few years and hung out in dark bars playing ska music and falling in love with travel, good food and local drink.

ABOUT THE PUBLISHER

Inkwell Media Services produces media content for publications and agencies across the music, travel, and winter sports platforms. We also handle talent booking and oversight for music venues and festivals. If your band needs a professional bio, electronic press kit, social media suite, or assistance in any other way relating to how to present your group and deal with media, promoters, and venues, we can help.

Stay tuned to the blog at www.timwenger.net for updates, ideas, and to share your thoughts.

ACKNOWLEDGEMENTS

Thank you to my wife Alisha, to my bandmates over the years: Brandon French, Scott Fowler, Chad Howard, Josh Cordova, Greg Bell, Travis Allen, Grayson Zane, to the crews at Colorado Music Buzz and Herman's Hideaway: Keith Schneider, Chris Murphy, Andrea Viarrial, Christopher Thomas, Kale Nelson, Mike Roth, and to everyone I've met through playing music, working in music, or loving music.

Thank you to Cian O'Shea at Korrection for editing, Alisha Williams for editing, and Kelly Claus Creative for formatting this book. I owe you all several beers.

Cover photo by Chandra Fowler

CPSIA information can be obtained
at www.ICGtesting.com
Printed in the USA
FSOW02n0754140517
34256FS

9 781684 185702